Living with an Angry Spouse

....

Help for Victims of Abuse

Edward T. Welch

New
Growth
Press

newgrowthpress.com

New Growth Press, Greensboro, NC 27401
Copyright © 2008 by Christian Counseling & Educational Foundation. All rights reserved. Published 2008

Cover Design: The DesignWorks Group, Nate Salciccioli and Jeff Miller, www.thedesignworksgroup.com

Typesetting: Robin Black, www.blackbirdcreative.biz

ISBN-10: 1-934885-35-5
ISBN-13: 978-1-934885-35-2

Library of Congress Cataloging-in-Publication Data

Welch, Edward T., 1953-
  Living with an angry spouse / Edward T. Welch.
      p. cm.
  Includes bibliographical references and index.
  ISBN 978-1-934885-35-2
 1. Abused women—Religious life. 2. Abusive men.
3. Violence in men. 4. Anger—Religious aspects—
Christianity. 5. Violence—Religious aspects—Christianity.
6. Family violence—Religious aspects—Christianity. I. Title.
  BV4596.A2W45 2008
    248.8'44—dc22

                                  2008011945
Printed in India

29 28 27 26 25 24 23 22   14 15 16 17 18

t shouldn't be.

You married someone you trusted, and you gave yourself to that person. How could it be that the person you once trusted with your life now acts like the person who could *take* your life? Whether you are facing unpredictable anger or outright physical abuse, this is betrayal at its worst.

It just shouldn't be.

You Are Not Alone

A quick scan of the internet reveals that you are certainly not alone. Twenty-five percent of adult women say they have experienced violence at the hands of their spouse or partner in a dating relationship. Men too can be victims of spousal violence. Eight percent report at least one such incident. But since men are more often violent against women, and since women are typically weaker than angry or violent men, this article is written especially for women.

If you have experienced violence and are living scared, statistics are not much comfort. Women who live in identical conditions don't protect you or give you hope for peace and reconciliation. But the numbers do remind you that others know the pain of such a living situation, and that resources are available to help you.

Where can you turn for help? Where can you find a wise friend to guide you? Do you attend a church? Talk to your pastor. If you don't attend a church, find one in your area. Look for a Bible-believing church that teaches that Jesus is the Son of God who came to earth, died for our sins, rose from the dead, and is the living and powerful head of his church today. Find a community of people who worship this Jesus and express their worship in love for one another. There you will find hope and direction. There you will hear about the God who hears.

You Are *Really* Not Alone: Listen to the God-Who-Hears

Your long-term goal should be to know the personal God. This won't magically change your situation, but you will find that knowing God does change everything. Think about it for a moment. What would it be like to know you're not alone, you're heard, and the one who hears is acting on your behalf? It would make a difference. It would especially make a difference if you knew that this person was the Holy King of the universe. The challenge, of course, is that right now you cannot see God with your eyes. When you want real hands and feet to help you, the knowledge of God's presence might seem to provide very little consolation, but don't let your senses mislead you. God's presence is a *real* spiritual presence. The Spirit will confirm this. "Blessed are those who have not seen and yet have believed" (John 20:29).

How do you know that the invisible God of the universe is with you? Look at the evidence from the past. The Bible is full of stories about God hearing the cries of his people and coming to their rescue. In Genesis, the first book in the Bible, a woman named Hagar and her young son were unfairly sent from their home and left in the wilderness to die. She turned her back on her son so she wouldn't have to watch him die, and they both wept. They thought they were utterly alone, but God heard them. This is what it says: "God heard the boy crying, and the angel of God called to Hagar from heaven and said to her, 'What is the matter, Hagar? Do not be afraid; God has heard the boy crying as he lies there. Lift the boy up and take him by the hand, for I will make him into a great nation'" (Genesis 21:17–18).

This is a pattern. God's ears are finely tuned to tears. Like a mother who wakes at the sound of her child, God hears the cries of the oppressed. We see this again when God's people, the Israelites, cried out because of their slavery in Egypt (Exodus 2:23–24). Like Hagar, the people were not even crying out to God; they were simply crying, and God heard. Some people can hear and do nothing, but when the God of heaven and earth hears, he acts. He gave Hagar and her son water and made her son the father of a great nation. He responded to the cries of the Israelites by delivering them from their slavery in Egypt.

So don't think that God merely listens. His listening always includes action. We may not see all of what he is doing, but, make no mistake, he is acting.

You Are Not Alone: The God-Who-Hears Wants to Listen to You

And there is more. God wants to hear *you*. He wants you to direct your cries and fears to him. Does that seem impossible? If so, he will help you to find the words. Psalm 55 can get you started:

My heart is in anguish within me; the terrors

of death assail me. Fear and trembling have beset me; horror has overwhelmed me. I said, "Oh, that I had the wings of a dove! I would fly away and be at rest—I would flee far away and stay in the desert; I would hurry to my place of shelter, far from the tempest and storm."...If an enemy were insulting me, I could endure it; if a foe were raising himself against me, I could hide from him. But it is you, a man like myself, my companion, my close friend, with whom I once enjoyed sweet fellowship as we walked with the throng at the house of God. (Psalm 55:4–8, 12–14)

Psalm 55 has given a voice to human betrayal for centuries. If the words fit your experience, then you are now part of a much larger body of people who have sung this psalm and made it their own. One person in particular leads the singing. Yes, King David wrote this psalm, but he wrote it on behalf of the perfect King who was to come after him. It is Jesus' psalm, and they are his words you're sharing in. He was *the* innocent victim of evil people. He was betrayed, tortured, and suffered a terrible death at their hands (Mark 14—15). To be part of his chorus, all you have to do is follow him.

Indeed, you are not alone.

Keep Listening: The God-Who-Hears Is Against Injustice

The God who came to this world as Jesus and experienced oppression and injustice also stands against it. When people are oppressed by those who have authority or physical power, God pronounces grief and judgment on the oppressors.

> "Woe to the shepherds who are destroying and scattering the sheep of my pasture!" declares the Lord. Therefore this is what the Lord, the God of Israel, says to the

shepherds who tend my people: "Because you have scattered my flock and driven them away and have not bestowed care on them, I will bestow punishment on you for the evil you have done," declares the LORD. "I myself will gather the remnant of my flock out of all the countries where I have driven them and will bring them back to their pasture, where they will be fruitful and increase in number." (Jeremiah 23:1–3)

This doesn't mean you should silently gloat, *Yeah, go ahead. You'll get yours someday.* As you probably know, women who are victimized usually don't think like that. It's more likely that you feel guilty, as if somehow you are the cause of judgment on your spouse. But neither response is what God intends. He wants you to respond by depending on him to be your defender. He wants you to trust that he is hearing your cries and is going to act on your behalf.

Practical Strategies for Change

Most likely, you are numb, scared, confused, and paralyzed. If this describes you, then you might know some action steps, but taking one will seem impossible. There is no trick to taking a first step; you just have to do it. Start by making a phone call to your pastor or a friend. You need help, and God's hands and feet often are the friends he raises up to help you. Look for God's help to arrive from God's people.

You have many reasons why you don't ask for help. One is that you don't know exactly what kind of help you need. For example, you aren't eager for someone to confront your husband because you are afraid he will get even angrier at you. You don't want to leave. So what's left to do? Your path isn't clearly marked, and you're not sure what to do next. That makes it even more important for you to ask for help from someone else.

Another reason you might not ask for help is because you are experiencing something shameful. Here's the question in the back of your mind: What kind of wife gets treated this badly by her husband? Your (wrong) answer? Only a bad wife could elicit such a response from someone sworn to love her.

The truth is that someone else's cruel anger is not your fault. Even if you incite it, and that is rarely the case, there is *never* any excuse for cruelty. Put it this way: You can't make someone else sin. Sin comes from our own selfish hearts. Your spouse, when he is sinfully angry, is caring only about himself and his own desires (James 1:13–15). He will try to make it sound like it's your fault—there isn't a victimized woman in the world who doesn't feel like she is somehow at fault—but his sin is his alone.

If Necessary, Find Refuge

If you have been physically hurt by your spouse, and he continues to threaten you, then you should get protection. If children are threatened, this is essential. Every county in the United States has domestic abuse hot lines that will provide you with resources. Protection from abuse orders are available though your local courthouse. Friends have an extra room or two. If you choose to leave, that is not necessarily a first step toward divorce. It is better understood as a statement of hope and a desire to see change in the marriage relationship.

The Bible emphasizes that marriage is a covenant that should not be broken unless we have God's permission (Matthew 19:6). Do you have permission when there is domestic violence? This is a difficult question which you should not try to answer on your own. But know this for certain: God opposes such evil and intends care for the oppressed (Jeremiah 23:1–3). Such care can sometimes be found in finding a place for refuge and protection.

Listen to the Advice of Wise Friends

As you think through the difficult decisions about how to keep you and your children safe, you need to ask your pastor and other wise people who love Jesus to talk to you and guide you. Decisions about your marriage should not be made alone. God's wisdom says that the more important the decision, the more critical it is to receive counsel from other wise people.

The reality is that most women who are suffering as you are don't take these steps. Some women who *do* take these steps quickly renege on them and go back to the abusive situation. Why? Fear of retaliation, fear of aloneness, love for the perpetrator, hope that things at home will change, and the lingering guilt that says it's your fault. These are powerful tugs that make decisive action very difficult. With this in mind, the decision is, of course, your own, but you can see how important it is to listen for the consensus among the wise people around you. If you have fears and doubts about their counsel, voice them.

Be Guided by Love

Here's a hard distinction, but it can go a long way toward bringing you sanity. Have you noticed that in all relationships we balance our commitment to love with our desire to be loved? Usually the scales are tipped in favor of wanting to be loved. Your goal is to tip the scales towards a commitment to love. This is the way to avoid the twin contaminants of most relationships: anger and fear. When you *need* someone more than you love that person, you will be prone to anger, because you don't get the love that feels so critical to you. You will also be prone to fear, because the other person has the power to give or withhold what you think you need.

When you set your sights on love, the possibilities are limitless. Love gives you the clarity to make difficult decisions on the fly. Should you speak out or be quiet? Love can guide you more than you realize. Even going to someone else and asking for advice and help with your difficult relationship can be an expression of love. You need help because you care about your partner. His foolish, selfish lifestyle is not only hurting you, it's also hurting him because it's spiritually self-destructive. Real love wants to warn the fool. It wants to rescue, if it is at all possible, the self-destructive person from the wrath of God.

Love can be patient and kind (1 Corinthians 13). It can rebuke (Leviticus 19:17). It can stand against injustice and confront another person in their sin (Matthew 18:15–17). The challenge is to keep the scales tipped in love's favor.

You can only do this when you remember that God always tips the scales in love's favor in his relationship with you. No matter how moral you have been, you have not been perfectly faithful to the one who created you. But instead of withdrawing in anger, he pursues you, even when you don't want to be pursued. Find the Book of Hosea in your Bible (it's in the Old Testament), and read the first three chapters. You will get a picture of God as the relentless lover of his people. Although his people repeatedly reject him, he will not give them up or let them go.

As you know and experience God's pursuing love, your love for others, including your spouse, will become stronger than your desire to be loved. Trusting in God's love will free you to love others the way you have been loved. After all, when we were God's enemies, he extended his call of love to us (Romans 5:10). Since God loved us like that, we should expect that we will have the opportunity to love others in the same way. The Bible calls this overcoming evil with good (Romans 12:21).

What to Do When Your Spouse Is Angry

Outfitted with love you have more power than you think. Love comes from the Spirit of the living God, the same Spirit who raised Jesus from the dead, and whenever you encounter the Spirit in the Bible, you encounter power. The power, of course, is the power of wisdom and love, and there are times when it can disarm an angry man.

Because of the limitless possibilities of love, let wise friends brainstorm and pray with you. Here are some things that the Spirit of power can help you do when you are faced with an angry spouse:

- Ask him why he thinks you are the enemy.
- Leave the house when he is sinfully angry.
- Go and get help instead of being silenced by your shame and his threats.
- Accept responsibility for your own sinful responses, but don't accept responsibility for his.
- Tell him what it is like to be the recipient of his anger and hatred. Angry people are blind to how they hurt others.
- Ask him if he thinks that he has a problem.

- Speak with a humility that's more powerful than anger. When in doubt, you could ask what he thinks you did that was wrong. You don't have to defend your reputation before him.
- If he claims to want to change, ask him what steps he is taking to change.
- Keep James 4:1–2 in mind. You are witnessing his selfish desires running amok. Be careful that you don't become an imitator of such behavior.
- Don't minimize his destructive behavior. Sinful anger is called hatred and murder (Matthew 5:21–22).
- Read through the Book of Proverbs underlining all the sayings about anger. Proverbs like "reckless words pierce like a sword" will validate your experiences (Proverbs 12:18).
- Remember, it is possible to overcome evil with good.

This is only a sketchy map. The details will have to be worked out within your community of counselors. What guarantees do you have? God doesn't guarantee the momentary peace and quiet you might be longing for; instead, he promises you something much more lasting. He promises that, as you turn and trust Jesus Christ, you will become more like him; that his Spirit will help you love more than you need to be loved; that God will be with you, he will hear and act on your behalf; and that, although the Spirit of God is the one who changes hearts, you have more power than you know—the power to both know and promote peace.

A Plan for Change

Can an angry, abusive spouse change?

Most women who are living in an abusive relationship are waiting and hoping for their husband to change. But you haven't seen that happen, yet. You might be thinking, *He has promised to change so many times, but we end up at the same*

place. Can he change, or is there a deeper problem?
Sin is hard to leave, in part, because we like it. In
the case of abusive anger, the angry person might
like the sense of power and control he thinks his
anger gives him.

Is it possible for God to change lifelong pat-
terns of anger and violence? The answer is yes,
absolutely! God changes all kinds of people. If he
can change us, when we see that our hearts are
prone to selfishness and quickly stray from trusting him, then he can certainly change people who
are like us. So don't reject your husband if he says
he wants to change. Instead, talk with him about
whether or not he is willing to take the necessary
steps that would lead to change. If he is serious
about changing, he needs to have a plan. This
plan should include at least the following things:

- *Accountability:* He must be willing and able
  to speak openly about his sinful behavior
  to others who can help.

- *Confession:* He must be able to understand and confess that his anger has been destructive, recognize that his behavior is ultimately against God, and learn to hate his sin.
- *Growth in the knowledge of the true God:* All the best intentions are not enough to bring about deep change. The real problem with angry men is their arrogance and "hatred toward God" (James 4:1–10), in which case they must confess their sin against God and set out on a course of knowing and fearing him.

Put Your Hope in God

You probably already believe that God has the power to change anyone. Your biggest struggle will be to put your hope in God more than you put your hope in your husband changing. When you put your hope in God, you live on a rock.

When you put your hope in a person, you will feel like a life raft let loose on the open sea. Set your hope on the God who hears you. Look to him for deliverance and the power to love, and you will not be disappointed (2 Corinthians 1:10).

Simple, Quick, Biblical

Advice on Complicated Counseling Issues
for Pastors, Counselors, and Individuals

MINIBOOK
CATEGORIES

- Personal Change
- Marriage & Parenting
- Medical & Psychiatric Issues
- Women's Issues
- Singles
- Military

USE YOURSELF | GIVE TO A FRIEND | DISPLAY IN YOUR CHURCH OR MINISTRY

New
Growth
Press

Go to **newgrowthpress.com** or call **336.378.7775** to
purchase individual minibooks or the entire collection.
Durable acrylic display stands are also available to house
the minibook collection.